Doing What's Right

Jan Black, Author

Steve Hunt and Dave Adamson, Design and Illustration

We, the people what made this book,
like to help kids do what is right.

And the One who helped all of us was God,
Who wants even more than we do to help
you do what is right.

To enable Christian educators and schools worldwide to effectively prepare students for life

© 1985 The Association of Christian Schools International. Adapted by permission from materials formerly copyrighted by Christian School Curriculum, a division of Fleming H. Revell Company. Reprinted 1997, 2000.

All rights reserved. No portion of this book may be reproduced in any form without prior written permission of the Association of Christian School International.

Publishing is a function of the Academic Affairs Department of ACSI. As an organization, ACSI is committed to the ministry of Christian school education, to enable Christian educators and schools worldwide to effectively prepare students for life. As a publisher of books, textbooks, and other resources, ACSI endeavors to produce biblically sound materials that reflect Christian scholarship and stewardship, and that address the identified needs of Christian schools around the world.

For additional information, write ACSI, Academic Affairs Department, PO Box 35097, Colorado Springs, CO 80935-3509.

Scripture taken from THE HOLY BIBLE, NEW INTERNATIONAL VERSION. Copyright © 1973, 1978, 1984 by the International Bible Society. Used by permission of Zondervan Bible Publishers. All Rights Reserved.

Printed in the United States of America

Character Foundation Textbook Series-Doing What's Right Student Edition
ISBN *1-58331-142-4* **Catalog # *7027***

Association of Christian Schools International
PO Box 35097 • Colorado Springs, CO • 80935-3509
Customer Service: 800/367-0798 • Website: http://www.acsi.org

Table of Contents

2 1 3
Things God wants me to
Remember

1. Love God

2. Love others

3. Do right

4

'Fridge ♥ Friend
ACTIVITY SHEET

Dear First-Grade Families!

You have just started reading your first FRIDGE FRIEND letter. It came out of a new book that we opened this week called, DOING WHAT'S RIGHT.

DOING WHAT'S RIGHT is a book that our school is using as a tool for character development. We want to assist you in helping your child learn to make right choices, and we are delighted to do it in this creative and practical way.

You will receive several letters similar to this one during the school year. They will tell you of the latest goings-on in the world of first grade character development. They will also keep you up-to-date on the adventures of Miss Dandee's first grade classroom at the foot of Half-Pint Hill. But best of all, they will give you an opportunity to share a few important minutes with your child as you complete the Activity Sheet on the back of each letter.

The letter and activity sheet are called FRIDGE FRIENDS because we hope that is what they will become in your home. By displaying them openly on your refrigerator door, you are satisfying several critical needs:

First, you are applauding your child's efforts and showing interest in his/her life.
Second, you are reinforcing an important life concept.
Third, you are strengthening a memory of time spent with you.

We are grateful to be an avenue of influence in the life of your child. God bless you as you trust Him to help you live your life DOING WHAT'S RIGHT. We pray often for His best in your life.

Sincerely,

Your Child's Teacher

This Month's Chracter Qualities:
Wisdom: Thinking God's Way.
Obedience: Doing What I Am Told.

Verse we are learning in class:
"Children, obey your parents in everything for this pleases the Lord."   Col.3:20

A Look at Leaves

Have you ever heard of a leaf factory?   Have you ever seen a leaf machine?
Have you ever met a leaf painter? No? That's because God makes them all by
Himself. He doesn't use His hands to make leaves.   He uses His mouth. How?
He just speaks and the leaf is there.

A Poem to Learn Together:

I picked up a leaf and what did I see?
I saw tiny hints that God loves me.
I smelled its blossom in the spring,
I felt its shade in summer green.
I watched it turn from green to gold,
I saw it fall as it was told.
I heard it scrunch beneath my feet,
I watched it twirl across my street.
I felt it touch me where I stood,
I knew why God said, "It is good."

God, we think you are great for making a leaf out of nothing!

We're going to have a Leaf Celebration next week. Please bring to class four of the
prettiest leaves you can find. Thank you.

"Parents are the pride of their children."
Proverbs 17:6

Wisdom

Thinking God's Way	Thinking Like A Fool

Wisdom comes from God
Prov. 2:6

Wisdom helped God make the world.

Think about that for 30 seconds.

```
 1   2   3   4   5   6   7   8   9   10
11  12  13  14  15  16  17  18  19  20
21  22  23  24  25  26  27  28  29  30
```

Wisdom will help you, too.

God says that if you love wisdom, wisdom will love you.

Draw something to show what you are thinking about wisdom.

7

Wisdom Wins!

The Thinking Page

Thinking happens to all of us.

Think! 1 2 3 4 5 6 7 8 9 10

What do you think?

Thinking can move ◇◇◇◇◇◇◇ and ◇◇◇◇◇◇◇

Thinking can

Thinking can make us feel _____
Thinking can make us feel _____

God wants our thinking to be good for us.

God says He will help us train our minds to think right if we ask Him.

What do you think about that?

8

The Smart Thinking Page

It is smart to think about God.
Let's think about God now. Ready? Begin!

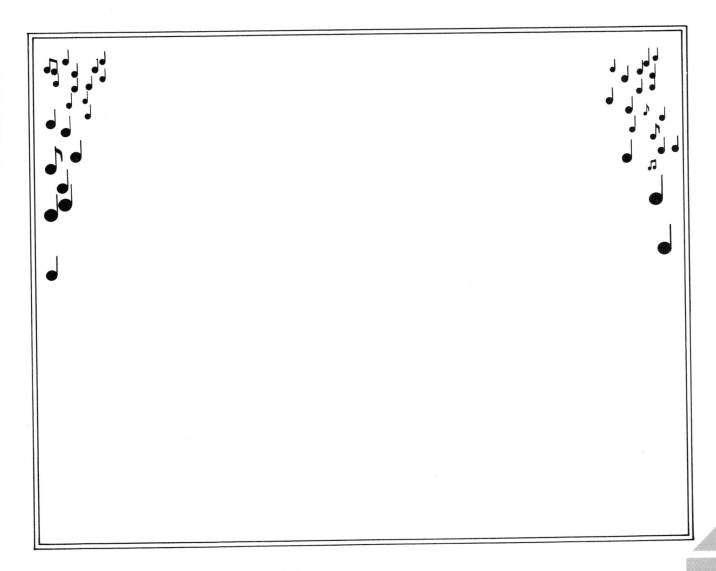

I think, "Wow"!

Thinking God's Way

Wisdom will help you think God's way.
Can you think God's way through this map?

If you love wisdom, wisdom will love you.
Proverbs 8:17

Wisdom Wins!

We have been Thinking

About God:

_____

- - - - - - - - - - - - - - - - -

_____

About wisdom:

_____

- - - - - - - - - - - - - - - - -

_____

About doing right:

_____

- - - - - - - - - - - - - - - - -

_____

This is what we think.
What do you think about what we think?

God wants me to have wisdom.
I can ask for wisdom.
James 1:5
I can learn wisdom by knowing how God thinks.
Proverbs 9:10

Be thinking of a Q.

11

Obedience

Obey

Doing what I am told	Not doing what I am told

Obedience pleases God.

"Children, _____ your parents in everything, for this pleases the Lord." Colossians 3:20

A fun little
obedience check-up

"I will obey your Word!"
Psalm 119:17b

I Did Well!

☆

13

Obey Today!

Who tells you what to do?
How do they tell you what to do?

Thinking God's Way,
Why do you need to be told what to do?

My Obedience

My obedience pleases God.

When I do what I am told, I give a gift to God that will never wear out.

Thinking God's way is

wise

14

Noah, the Grown-up Obeyer

Obeying was hard for Noah.
But obeying was good for him.

Obeying can be hard.
But obeying is good for me.

Joey, the First Grade Obeyer

First graders are good obeyers.
Joey is a first-grade obeyer.

Hard to obey:  Easy to obey: ___

Obedience is my  to God.
My  of obedience makes God

Attentiveness

Knowing what is going on	Not knowing what is going on

God pays attention to me.

"You (God) know when I sit and when I rise."

Psalm 139:2

I can pay attention to God and others.

A pay attention check-up

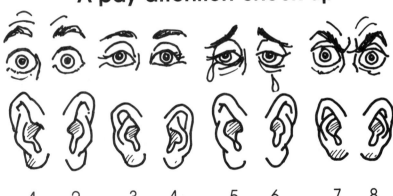

1   2   3   4   5   6   7   8

Can you pay attention?

_____ Yes, I can pay attention!

17

Attention!

Wigglers and Sleepyheads

These are wiggles. ~~~

Do you have some ~~~ ?

These are sleepies. z

Do you have some z-z-z ?

All of us get ~~~ and z-z-z

This is a room.
Please fill it with ~~~

This is a room.
Please fill it with z-z-z

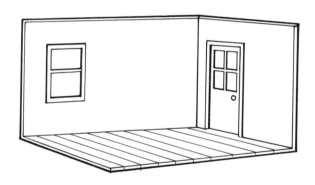

Can ~~~ and z-z-z ever be told
to leave? When?

God understands wiggles and sleepies. Why?
God asks us to learn to say "no" to them
sometimes.

'Fridge Friend
ACTIVITY SHEET

Dear First-Grade Families!

Attentiveness is on the character development agenda this month. We are discovering that paying attention is smart. When we know what is going on, we are able to choose what to do with what is happening. Plus we are finding out that many important surprises are in store for the person who pays attention to the big and little pieces of life.

How can adults encourage attentiveness in children? The best way is by being attentive themselves. Other ways to encourage attentiveness in children are:

1. Trigger curiosity with comments like, "I wonder how that works," or "Isn't that something!"
2. Pay attention to your surroundings. Note things like colors, blends of textures, aromas, moods, reactions, temperature. Verbalize your observations.
3. Have fun with short quizzes and games about the things around you, past adventures, Grandma's house, dreams for the future, paying close attention to detail.
4. Praise any amount of attentiveness in your child. "You really paid attention to the colors of that bird, didn't you!" "I noticed you were listening carefully to the coach's words today. That will be a big help to you."

But what about wiggles? Can wiggles and attentiveness find mutual fulfillment within the body walls of a first-grader? Occasionally. Through the use of games with timers and stopwatches we are encouraging short, wiggle-free attentiveness now and then. Some light-hearted reinforcement and honest praise at home would double the impact.

The second quality we will be studying is FAITH. The definition is "Believing God." According to Jesus, children have the leading edge in faith. They are Faith Champions, and we can learn from their example.

So there you have it: Attentiveness linked with Faith, adding further strength to the character of your child. We are glad to be in on the wonder of it all.

Sincerely,

Your Child's Teacher

This Month's Character Qualities:
Attentiveness: Knowing what is going on.
Faith: Believing God

Verse we are learning in class:
"My son, pay attention to what I say; listen closely to my words. Do not let them out of your sight, keep them within your heart." Proverbs 4:20, 21

19

Attention!

God is paying attention to me right now!

These are verses with missing vowels. We found the vowels for you and put them in order. Copy the vowels from the list into the spaces. You will find out one thing God is doing.

o o e l i a e l i e o e e i e o u o a a o e i o u o e a e o u o u O
o o a i e u o e e e l o o u e e o u o u u e e a i o a

"Y__u Kn__w wh__n __ s__t __nd
wh__n __ r__s__; y__u p__rc__ __v__
my th____ghts fr__m __f__r. H__w
pr__c____s t__ m__ __r__ y__ __r
th____ghts, __ G__d! H__w v__st __s
th__ s__m __f th__m!
   W__r__ __ t__ c____nt th__m,
th__y w____ld ____tn__mb__r th__
gr____ns __f s__nd."

That was a lot of work! There were a lot of vowels missing. Just think, God has had more thoughts about you today than even the number of missing vowels!

Wondering Together

I wonder what God is thinking about me right now.
I wonder what kind of a person He thinks I am.
I wonder what God likes best about me.
I wonder what God would like me to do better.
I wonder if He can hardly wait for me to get to heaven.
I wonder.

I can pay attention to God

I can think about Him. And I will.

My thinking space.

My reading and listening space

I can read about Him or listen to words about Him. And I will.

I can talk about Him. And I will.

My talking space.

21

Faith

God keeps His promises.

I Cor. 1:9

Go, Champ!

God is Faithful.

_____

- -

_____

Our list of what God says.

1. I am the only God. Isaiah 43:11
2. I love people. John 3:16
3. I forgive sin. I John 1:9
4. I see you. Psalm 139:3,17
5. I hear you. Psalm 34:6
6. I made the earth. Genesis 1:1
7. I am saving a place for you in heaven. John 14:6
8. I will help you. Isaiah 40:31

Go, Champ!

The Hands and Feet of Faith

Believing God will do what He says makes my hands and feet do special things.

This is my hand of faith.   This is my foot of faith.

This is my mouth of faith.

Go, Champ!

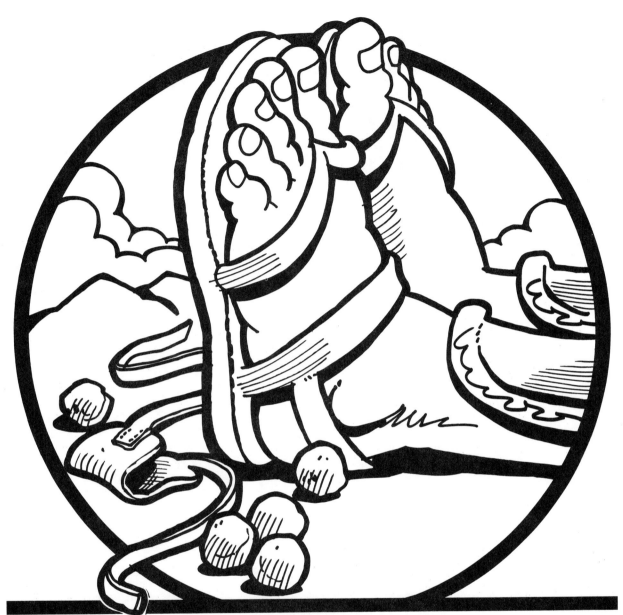

I'm a Champ

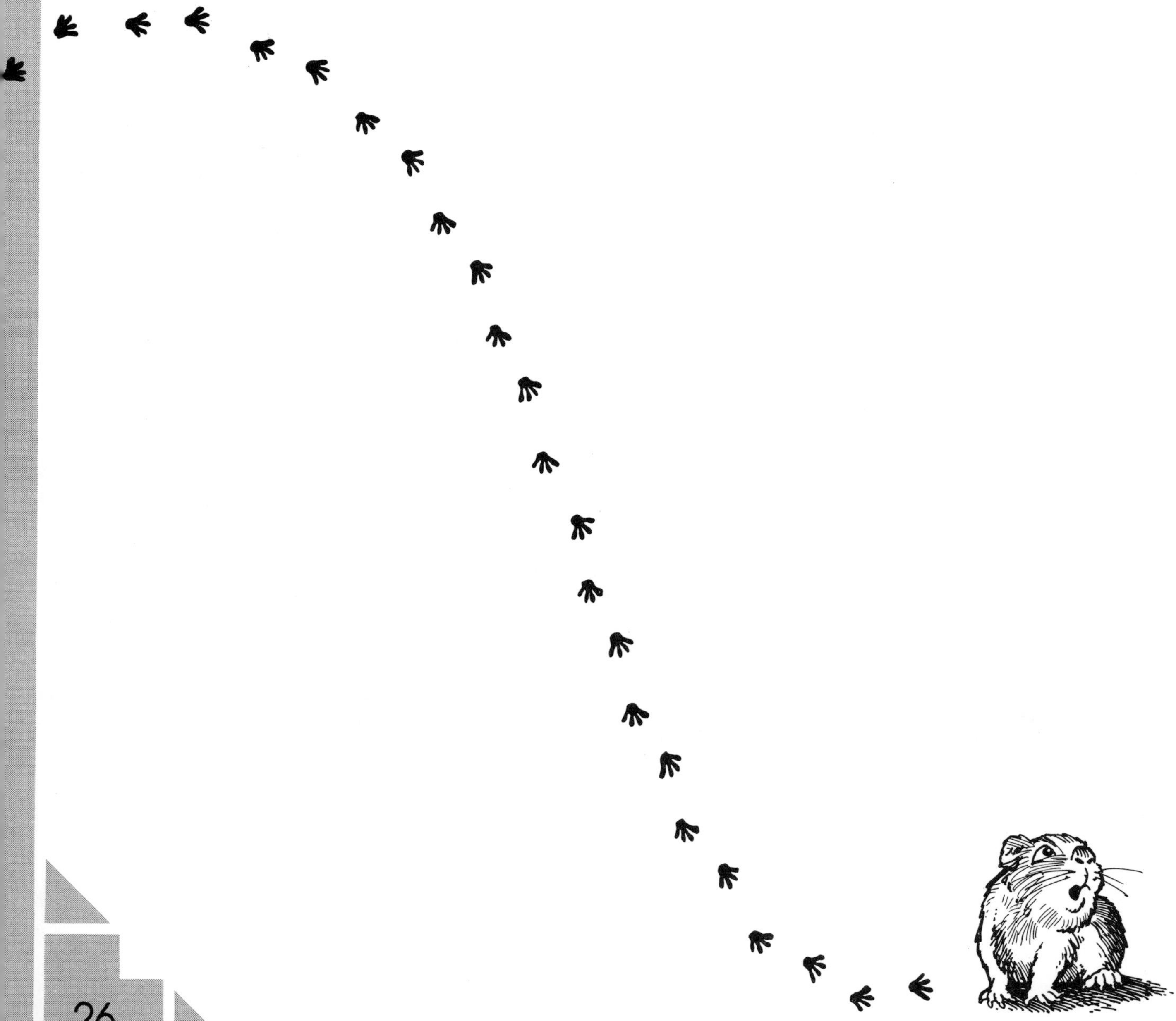

Thankfulness

Thanks
Grateful

Thinking and saying thanks.	Complaining.

Being thankful is wise and right.
In everything give _____

I Thessalonians 5:18

My very own kind of thank-you list:

Think Thanks!

The Never-Say-Thank-You Girl

28

'Fridge ♥ Friend
ACTIVITY SHEET

Dear First Grade Families!

Happy Thanksgiving. It will come as no surprise to you that Thankfulness is one of the two qualities emphasized this month in our book, *Doing What's Right*. Orderliness is the second quality.

Expressing gratitude has the ability to change lives. The life of the thanks-giver is brightened, and the load of the thanks-receiver is lightened.

Saying thank-you to children for specific effort and improvement reinforces their desire to repeat the action. However, many times it is difficult for parents to know what to notice and how to say it.

For that reason, we have listed some basic words of thanks applicable to most first graders. You will want to tailor them to your needs:

"I'm pleased with the way you are keeping your hair combed."

"You have been keeping your voice down today. Thanks very much. It really helps, especially when the baby is asleep."

"I was watching you play with your friends. They may not say it, but I am sure they are thankful for a friend like you. I know I am."

"Those hugs you give me in the morning seem to make my day start better. Thanks for remembering to give me one."

"I'm so thankful for your giggles."

We hope that as you dwell for a time on thankfulness that you will let God open your eyes to all that He has provided, especially in giving you the privilege of spending life with a child.

Gratefully,

Your Child's Teacher

This month's character qualities:
Thankfulness: Thinking and saying thanks.
Orderliness: Keeping things in their place.

Verse we are learning in class:
"In everything give thanks, for this is God's will for you in Christ Jesus." I Thessalonians 5:18

Think Thanks!

Hang a pencil near this Fridge Friend so that the thankful thing you are thinking can be quickly written down during the remainder of the month. At Thanksgiving dinner you may want to read the list together then place it in a spot that is safe for memories.

THANKSGIVING

THANKS BE
TO GOD

Think Thanks!

Our Thank you Song

Think Thanks!

Orderliness

Keeping things in their place	Letting things get all mixed up.

Being neat is a help to me, to God, and to others.

But

_____

should

_____

in a

_____

and

_____

I Corinthians 14:40

Which line is the most orderly?

32

Neat is Nice!

God is Known for His Orderliness

This does not mean He fusses when we jump into a pile of His leaves. It means that He planned things in an orderly way. The things God made work together.

The ocean is a good, orderly place.

God is orderly, but He is not afraid of messes. Orderliness does not mean I can never have any fun getting messy.

33

My Perfectly Orderly Drawer

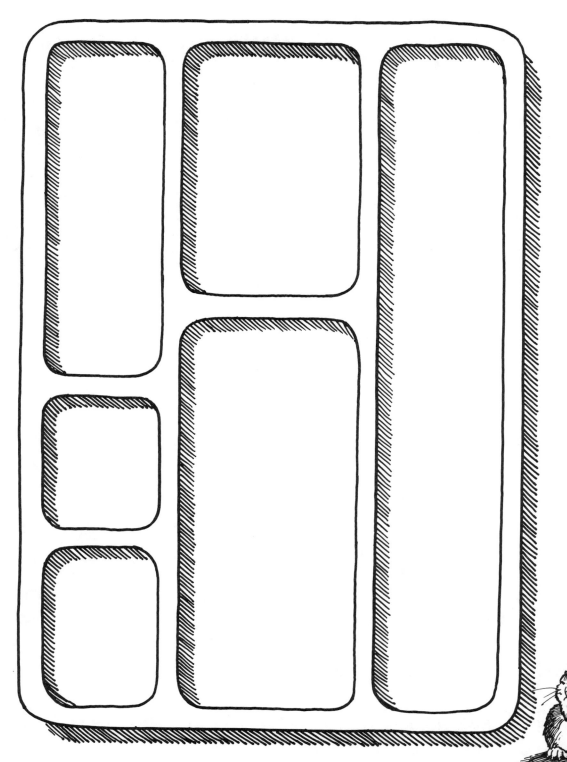

Neat is Nice!

35

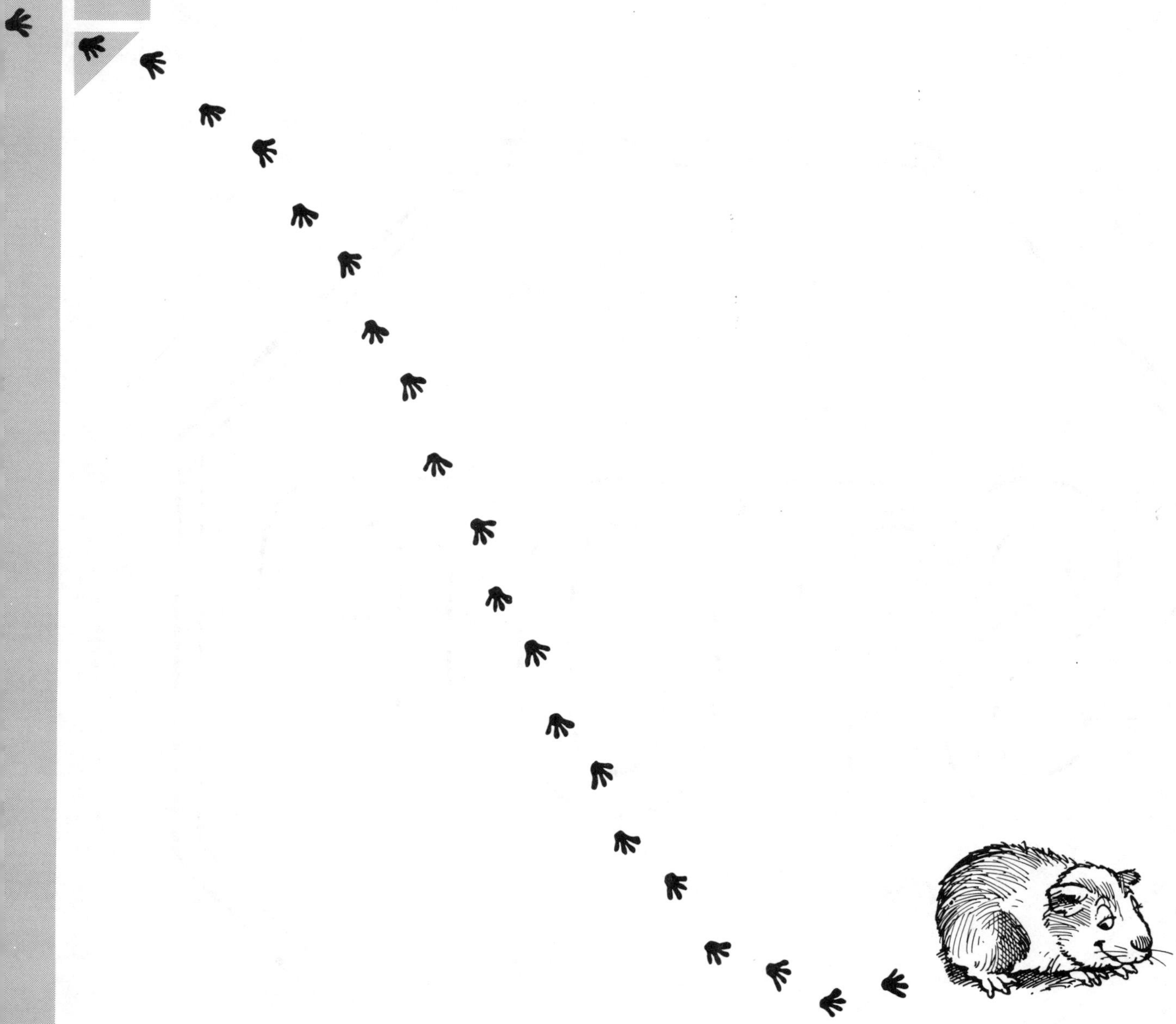

Meekness

Humility

Letting others be special, too.	Thinking I am most special.

God is most special.

A 's de

  +  low

but a  it

 ~~B~~ob+~~s~~tain

 honor. — Proverbs 29:23

Say it until you know it. How many times did it take you to learn it?

1 2 3 4 5 6 7 8 9 10 11 12 13 14 15 16 17 18 19 20

37

Others, too!

The God who came to Earth

Jesus gave up heaven for a few years
so that we could share it with Him forever.

Jesus showed meekness.

Others, too!

'Fridge ♥ Friend
ACTIVITY SHEET

Dear First-Grade Families!

The usual happenings at Christmas are taking place in our first grade class. There are decorations transforming the walls as well as our moods. There are secrets being whispered about gifts and parties and surprises. There is also talk of a different way of looking at Christmas.

Meekness and Loyalty are the two traits we are learning about in our character development emphasis for December. They become even more beautiful under the lights of Christmas.

Meekness is seeing yourself accurately and sharing the spotlight, so to speak. Jesus did more than that by giving up the glory of heaven for the dust of earth.

Loyalty is seen as He endured great hardship and insult – even death – because of His loyalty to His Father.

These two qualities don't just dress up Christmas. They add a touch of beauty to *every* day.

We wish you more than a Merry Christmas. We wish you the joy of meekness and the blessing of loyalty, two strands of background gold which are subtly, yet tightly, woven around the arrival of God on earth that first Christmas.

God bless you,

Your Child's Teacher

This month's character qualities:
Meekness: Letting others be special too.
Loyalty: Doing right for someone I care about, no matter what.

Verse we are learning in class:
"A man's pride brings him low, but a humble spirit will obtain honor." Proverbs 29:23

Meekness and loyalty aren't featured in the Christmas ads, yet they are two of the best parts of the season. There are other lovely qualities that are easily missed, such as generosity, obedience, courage, friendship, and, of course, love.

One way you can remember these qualities as a family is to select a certain color of Christmas light to represent each one.

First, decide which qualities you most want to remember.
Next, match the quality with a color of light.
Finally, write your choices on these Christmas lights;
then color them appropriately.

**Reminders of the Character of God
brighten any season.**

The Kids in the Manger

Henry

Attentiveness

Judy

Loud voice

Singing

Suzy

Helping hand

Marsha

Acting

Eric

Courage

Juan

Quick feet

Todd

Strength

Shelly

41

Loyalty

Doing right for someone I care about no matter what.	Doing right for someone only if it is easy.

God's loyalty to us is forever.

A friend loves

Proverbs 17:17

42

Stick Together.

Royal Loyalty

Stick Together.

The Very Special Never-Before Gift

Think Back

Alone

Cry

Friend

Mad

1

2

3

4

5

What was the never-before gift that Corey received from Teddy?

44

The Toughest Chain Around

Stick together

Others, too

Stick together

Others, too

Stick together

Others, too

Self-control

I can choose to have self-control.

_____

- - - - - - - - - - - - - - - - - - -

_____

_____

- - - - - - - - - - - - - - - - - - -

_____

_____

- - - - - - - - - - - - - - - - - - -

_____

xxxxxxxxxxxxxxxxxxxxxxxxxxxx
xxxxxxxxxx
Proverbs _____:_____

Cross out the word SELF-CONTROL from these letter squares.

axSuyEtLvrFqu-piCKOmwNuuuTidRaiOpL

What is left after self-control is gone?

Be Choosey!

Daniel, the Gold Medal Chooser

When Daniel was a child, he practiced self-control. When he became a grown-up, his self-control was strong.

Daniel's Self Control

My Self Control

What if Daniel had not used his self-control?

Be Choosey!

'Fridge Friend
ACTIVITY SHEET

Dear First-Grade Families!

Self-control is the issue this month in our on-going study of character qualities.

The person we are focusing on as our example of strong self-control is Daniel. We have thought as far as our minds can stretch about the many muscles of self-control he had developed.

He had chosen to study well and was known for his excellent knowledge.

He had taken care of himself physically and was appealing to the eye.

He had taken care to eat properly, knowing what was good for him.

He had developed the ability of maintaining successful relationships with authorities, as shown by approaches to the guard and the King.

He had chosen to do right above any consequence and stuck with his choice at great risk.

Muscle like this doesn't happen overnight. Daniel's self-control must have begun at a young age.

Daniel's self-control grew with him. He exercised it regularly. It enabled him to make tough decisions that were right.

In return for his self-control, Daniel received honor from God and had incredible influence on an entire nation.

Consider how Daniel's life would have been different had he pampered his self-control.

We have caught sight of the impact today's children can have on the world if they, as Daniel and his friends did, learn to develop a strong ability to be self-controlled and God-loving.

Please pray for us – and join with us – in exercising self-control in front of these young lives so that they can know what it looks like.

Sincerely,

Your Child's Teacher

This Month's Character Qualities:
Self-Control: Stopping myself before I do wrong.
Honesty: Saying and doing what is true.

Verse we are learning in class:
"A wise man keeps himself under control."
Prov. 29:11

Self-control

Exercise Chart

+ = I did it
⊗ = Oops!

Names of family members	Area to be strengthened	Progress marks

It is said that a craving or urge will leave in 90 seconds or less.
That means in just two minutes a new muscle
of self-control can appear!

Chooser Check-up

"Say, is your chooser working today?"

Each time the teacher makes the Sound of Self-Control, you choose one of these:

Sit		Stand
Front of room		Back of room
Say "duck"		Say "goose"
Tap your foot		Tap your fingers
Smile	or	Frown
Cough		Sneeze
Laugh loudly		Laugh quietly
Bend your knee		Bend your elbow
Sing "Row, Row, Row Your Boat"		Sing "Old MacDonald Had a Farm"

_____Yes, my chooser is working today.

_____No, my chooser is not working today.

51

Be choosey!

Honesty

| Saying and doing what is true. | Lying by what I say and do. |

Honesty pleases God and helps me.

"Each of you must _ _ _ _ _ _ _ _ _ _

_ _ _ _ _ _ _ _ _ _ _ _ _ _ _ _

and speak _ _ _ _ _ _ _ _ _ _

to his neighbor." Ephesians 4:25

Be Honest!

Today is:
THURSDAY

My
Mystery
Solving
Kit

Clues:_____

Ideas:_____

Wild guesses:_____

My choice for
Who did it_____

Do what's true.

An Honesty Think-in

Questions

Easier?

Scarier?

Best time?

Who?

How?

What if?

Hooray for the truth-telling God!

Do what's true.

55

Do what's true.

Diligence

Diligence makes me reliable.

Whatever
you do,
work at it
with all
your heart.
Colossians 3:23

CAREFUL WORK AHEAD

WARNING

57

Finish, friend.

Huff, Puff Do your Stuff

Dial Up Diligence

1	ABC 2	DEF 3
GHI 4	JKL 5	MNO 6
PRS 7	TUV 8	WXY 9
★	OPER 0	#

D i l i g e n c e

H a n g   i n   t h e r e

F i n i s h   t h e   j o b

D o n ' t   g i v e   u p

G o   f o r   t h e   G o l d

A code puzzle needing

___ ___ ___ ___ ___ ___ ___ ___ ___
4   9   12   9   7   5   14   3   5

Code

A-1 B-2 C-3 D-4
E-5 F-6 G-7 H-8
I-9 J-10 K-11 L-12
M-13 N-14 O-15
P-16 Q-17 R-18
S-19 T-20 U-21
V-22 W-23 X-24
Y-25 Z-26

___ ___ ___ ___ ___ ___ worked to get ready for ___ ___ ___ ___ ___ ___ .
10 15 19 5 16 8   6 1 13 9 14 5

___ ___ ___ ___ ___ worked hard to get out of ___ ___ ___ ___ ___ ___ ___ ___
13 15 19 5 19   5 7 25 16 20 7 15 4

___ ___ ___ ___ ___ ___ ___ ___ ___ ___
9 19 23 15 18 11 9 14 7 15 14

___ ___ ___ ___ ___ ___ ___ ___ ___ ___ .
21 19 23 9 20 8 12 15 22 5

Whew!

'Fridge Friend
ACTIVITY SHEET

Dear First-Grade Families!

With DILIGENCE and PATIENCE we are working our way through February. The word heard most often is FINISH. Tied for second-most-often are DO I HAVE TO? and YOU CAN DO IT!

Although there have been times of fun and games, the times have been tougher than usual. The students have had to think a bit longer and work harder to accomplish tasks such as those on the HUFF, PUFF, DO YOUR STUFF worksheet we recently completed.

Learning to finish the job with diligence and patience is a valuable asset. A young child can build a reputation as a finisher or as a quitter. We join you in your efforts to help your child be known as a finisher.

The Fridge Friend Activity Sheet this month is a Diligence Diary. You may adjust it to the needs of your family by using it in a variety of ways:

1. Make copies for individuals to use as personal diaries.

2. Select a job for the entire family to do together. Break it into steps that are easily accomplished and recorded.

3. Select several jobs to be done over the course of an evening, a Saturday, or a month. Check them off as they are finished.

4. When your choice is FINISHED, celebrate with a Diligence Dinner, carefully made by one or all the members of your Diligent Family!

As with all of the qualities we are studying, the importance of children seeing their adult models living out Diligence and Patience cannot be overstressed. We would appreciate your prayers as we patiently instruct. Be assured of ours for you as you patiently parent.

Sincerely,

Your Child's Teacher

This Month's Character Qualities:
Diligence: Working carefully until I am finished.
Patience: Waiting without complaining.

Verse we are learning in class:
"Whatever you do, work at it with all your heart, as working for the Lord, not for men." Colossians 3:23

Diligence Diary

Names: Job: Finished: (✔)

☐

☐

☐

☐

☐

☐

☐

☐

☐

☐

☐

☐

☐

☐

☐

Diligence Dinner Celebration: Date_____

What if God was a quitter?

Think through this thought from beginning

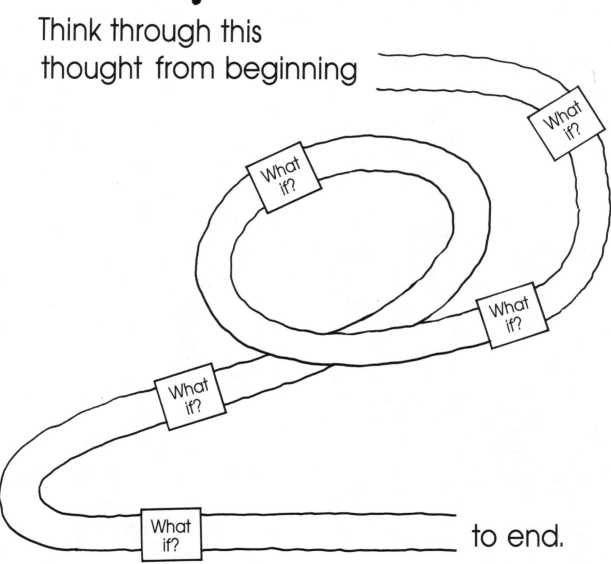

to end.

God is diligent. He finishes what He starts. He made you. He will stick with you. Remember, God is also loyal.

Finish, Friend.

Patience

Waiting without complaining	Wanting things right now!

God is patient with us.

Love is _____

I Corinthians 13:4

Patience, Pal.

How Long?

... can you wait for your friend to walk in tiny steps around the room?_____

... can you sit still?_____

... can you balance a pencil across your finger?_____

... can you wait to eat fried turkey bones covered with cheese sauce and popsicle juice?_____

... can you wait until your teacher hands out today's surprise?_____

Patience, Pal.

Slow Thomas, Patient Jesus

Do you know what these words mean?

slow	**believing**
alive	**loved**
patient	

Thomas was ___slow___ in ___believing___ that Jesus was ___alive___ again. Jesus ___loved___ Thomas. Love is ___patient___.

Patience, Pal.

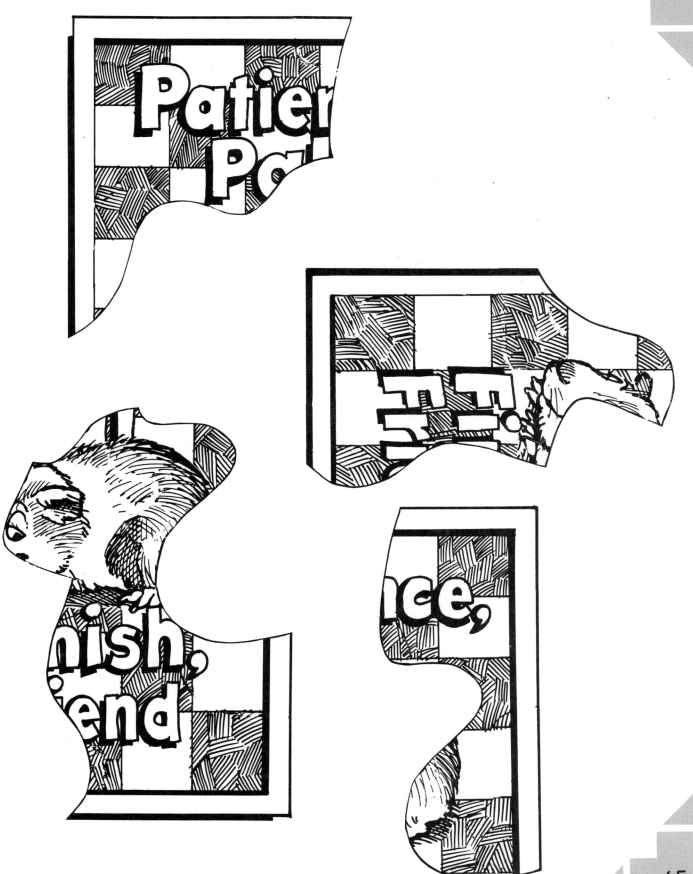

65

Forgiveness

Giving up my anger	Keeping my anger

God forgives me.

_____

_____ as the Lord

_____

_____ you! Colossians 3:14

Pouting   Making Up

                         Smiling

        Hugs   Second Chances

          Scary and Quiet Corner Sitting

    Slammed Doors   Words of Love

                 Tears of Joy

                                  Fast Driving

         Fighting

  Crying   Shouting

Forgiveness is God's good idea.

Forgive for God.

Mickey's Mad Mind

Forgive for God.

'Fridge ♥ Friend
ACTIVITY SHEET

Dear First-Grade Families!

Forgiveness is under investigation this month in DOING WHAT'S RIGHT, the character study we are continuing to enjoy.

The definition we are using is, "Giving up my hurt and anger toward a person." The opposite trait is, "Letting my hurt and anger stay with me." This can be a painful study, even for first graders.

Because we gather so much hurt by simply walking through a normal day, the subject of forgiveness is a practical one. When anger is added, forgiveness becomes even more crucial.

The perfect model of forgiveness is God. His promises of forgiveness are repeated throughout the Bible. He says He will take our dirty sins and make them white as snow. He will bury our sin in the depths of the sea, and will remember them no more. All of this is because of our trust in His Son, Jesus, who died to pay the bill for sin.

The Activity Sheet this month is a spin-off of the idea of God burying our sin. As you work through the ideas included in the Forgiveness Shovel, be conscious of any hurts or anger your child may have. We all know what pent-up anger does to a person's physical body. We see everyday what it does to relationships and job performance. Do your child a favor by patiently exampling forgiveness. Let your child see you confront issues and forgive offenses in a mature manner.

In the sixth chapter of Ephesians, Dads are warned not to exasperate their children. We as teachers and parents can easily – and unknowingly – do just that. It can be helpful to keep one another informed of any emotional mishaps that may occur in the teaching/parenting process.

Thank you for your continued support and encouragement to do what's right. We remain on your support team as well.

Sincerely,

Your Child's Teacher

This Month's Character Qualities:
Forgiveness: Giving up my anger.
Fairness: Showing kindness to all.

Verse we are learning in class:
"Forgive as the Lord forgave you." Colossians 3:13

God's Forgiveness Shovel

Think of it! God says He will bury your sin and forgive you!
Only a great God would do that.

Think of it! God says He will replace the anger you feel toward someone else with forgiveness.
Only a great God would do that.

Think of it! You get to choose to keep the anger you have for other people or bury it with God's shovel of forgiveness.

How?

By choosing to forgive those who have hurt you.
God says, "Forgive as the Lord forgave you."
It is your choice. But it is the only happy choice.

Who are you mad at? Think hard.
Will you forgive them?

Jesus said, "It is mine to avenge; I will repay."
God says to repay evil with good.

If you have decided to forgive someone who has hurt you, put a mark under the shovel on this page.
If you have told God you are sorry for a sin you have done, He has forgiven you. Put a mark under the shovel for each sin you have told God you are sorry for.
Add to the shovel with other marks of forgiveness during this month.

Forgiveness is God's Idea.
God has great ideas!

Peter's Mistake, God's Forgiveness

Peter did something we think we would never do. What did Peter do?

_____

- -

_____

Peter did something again that we think we would never do. What did Peter do again?

_____

- -

_____

Peter did something once more that we think we would never do. What did Peter do once more?

_____

- -

_____

Jesus did something we sometimes think He will not do. What did Jesus do?

_____

- -

_____

If we ever think God will not forgive us, we are not thinking God's way.

Peter was forgiven. Later, after Jesus returned to heaven, Peter wrote a book that is in the Bible. If you turn to I Peter 5:10, you will see one thing Peter wrote about God.

God loves you just like he loved Peter. Peter and God are together in heaven today because of God's forgiveness.

Forgive for God.

Fairness

Showing kindness to all	Showing kindness to only some

God always gives me a fair chance.

Love your neighbor as yourself. Rom. 13:9

There, there! Be fair!

Being fair is another way to be like Jesus.

There, there! Be fair!

Showing Favorites Again

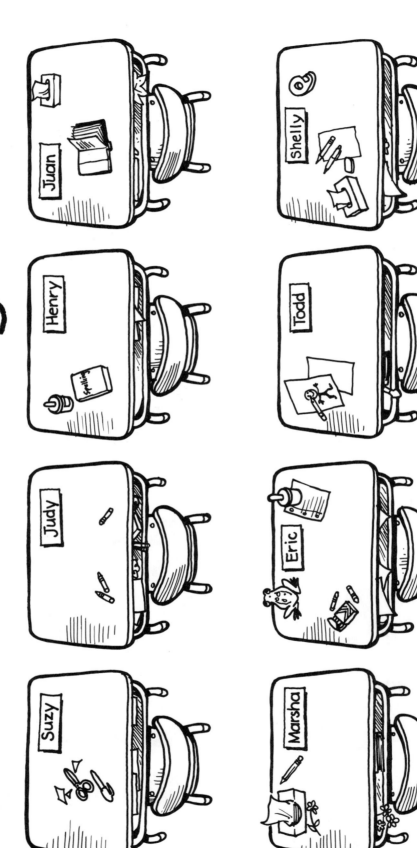

Thinking God's way, how should the lines look on this page?

There, there! Be fair!

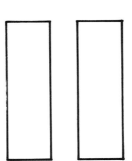

There, there! Be fair!

Initiative

Doing what I can to help	Leaving the helping to others

God finds ways to help us with our problems.

Each shape on this page has a twin. Use your initiative to help the shape twins wear the same words. If you do it right, you will have written some important words from the Bible about initiative.

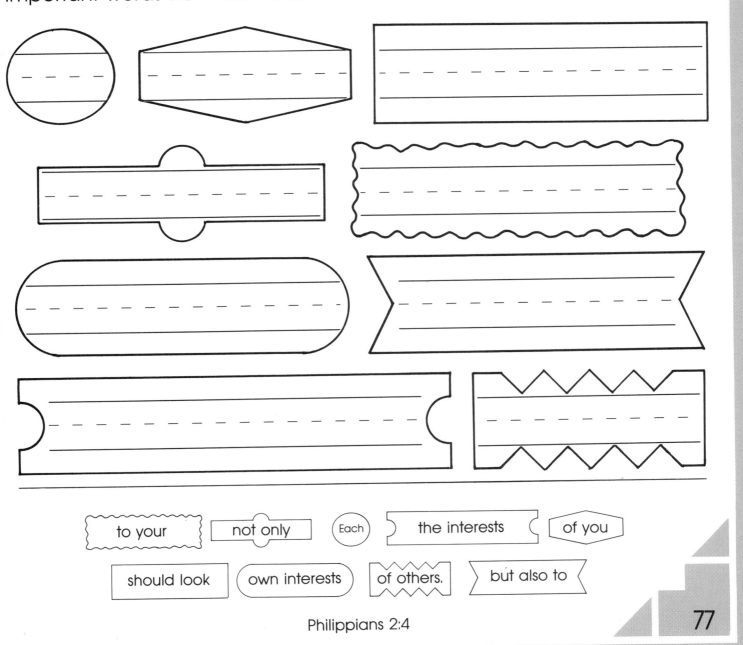

to your   not only   Each   the interests   of you

should look   own interests   of others.   but also to

Which Way Shall We Help?

The problem: Jesus had gone back to heaven. His friends, and others who believed Jesus was God, were taking good care of each other. Soon there were so many people that loved Jesus that the men who preached were spending too much time serving food and not enough time praying and preaching.

Using your **initiative**, decide what you would do to help fix this problem?

_____

- -

_____

_____

- -

_____

_____

- -

_____

_____

- -

_____

_____

- -

_____

To find out how the people used their initiative to solve their problem, find the book of Acts in your Bible. Your teacher will give you the exact spot to find the answer.

'Fridge ♥ Friend
ACTIVITY SHEET

Dear First-Grade Families,

"Hop To It!" is the slogan for INITIATIVE, one of the character qualities we are studying this month. Our focus is on seeing what needs to be done and then doing what we can to help.

In Miss Dandee's first grade class, students kept running out of pencils. Soon all kinds of initiative was activated and the result was a Pencil Party. Is there a need for help at your house? In the house of a friend? This would be a good time to find out and do something about it.

Some needs are simple: a hug, a note, a stack of cookies, a kind word.

Some needs are sort of simple: a ride to the store, packing up the garbage and taking it out, straightening a drawer, matching the socks, hand-washing a blouse.

Some needs are elaborate: babysitting for a day, sending a "care" package to grand-parents with goodies and love packed inside, cleaning a garage, sewing a dress, fixing dinner for an overworked or sick friend.

In your house today there is a young child who is eager to apply initiative to your needs. You are blessed. So are we by being on the receiving end of your child's unique and fresh view of life and its challenges.

Sincerely,

Your Child's Teacher

This Month's Character Qualities:
Love: Caring about others.
Initiative: Doing what I can to help.

Verses we are learning in class:
"Each of you should look not only to your own interests but also to the interests of others." Philippians 2:4

Teaming Up With Initiative

Here is the problem.	Here is our solution.
A problem we have ...	

My Helping God

God has ways of helping you with your problems. Some of them are hidden in the puzzle.

By coloring all of the shapes that have a dot in them, the missing parts will be found. Use them to fill in the sentences.

Ways God Helps Me

He ___ ___ ___ ___ ___ my call.

He ___ ___ ___ ___ ___   ___ ___ ___ ___ ___ when
I am hurting.

He ___ ___ ___ ___ ___ ___ ___ ___ over all who love Him.

Hop To It!

Love

Caring about others	Caring only about me

Love does what is best for the one we love.

In your fanciest writing, and no lines to guide you, write these words from God:

Love one another as I have loved you.
I John 15:12b

You may even want to write it in colors, since it does just happen to be God's idea of the second best thing you can ever do.****

****Thinking God's Way, and remembering way back to the first lesson, what is the **most important** thing we can do? _____

_____

Love cares.

It Was A Fight All Right!

Love cares.

God's Love Has No Finish Line

Love cares.

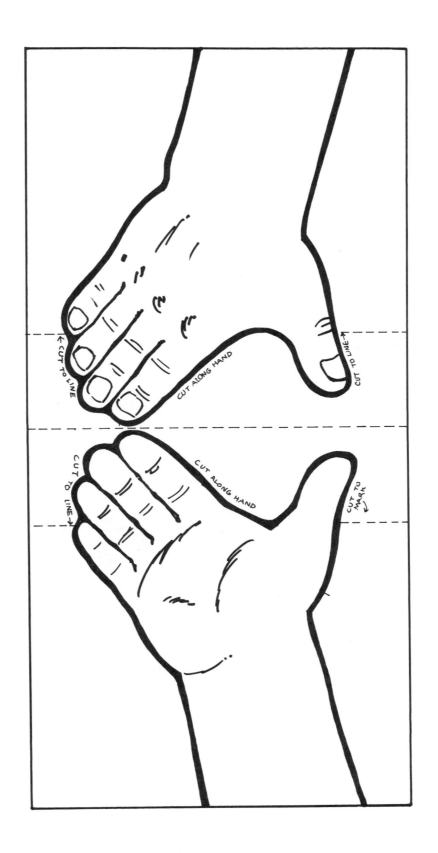

CUT TO LINE

CUT ALONG HAND

CUT TO LINE

CUT TO LINE

CUT ALONG HAND

CUT TO MARK

Love cares.

'Fridge Friend

ACTIVITY SHEET

Dear First-Grade Families!

You are holding the last Fridge Friend letter of the year. We are grateful for all that has taken place in the development of character in the children during the last nine months.

These last few lessons are focusing on DOING WHAT'S RIGHT. The unit looks back over things we have learned and looks ahead at things we can do beyond first grade in serving God and others.

The Activity Sheet on the back of this letter is a bit different in its approach this month. Instead of doing the activity WITH your child, we encourage you to do it FOR your child. Here's how:

Spend some thinking moments looking back over the year, noting progress that has been made in the area of character development. Find specific words of praise and growth to pass along to your child. Write them on the Activity Sheet and post it on the fridge for all the world to see.

Right now you have the greatest influence on the life of your child. As you capitalize on that privilege, you will have our continued prayers, help, and support.

Thank you for sharing in the life of our school through your child this year. God bless you all.

Sincerely,

Your Child's Teacher

Verse we are learning in class:
"Never tire of doing what is right."
2 Thessalonians 3:13

Let it be known
to all who enter this home that

has grown in character since September.

Here is proof:

Let it further be known to all who enter this home that the family of

is pleased to share a roof and a life with such a wonderful person.
Furthermore, we declare our forever love.

Signed: _____

Dated: _____

90

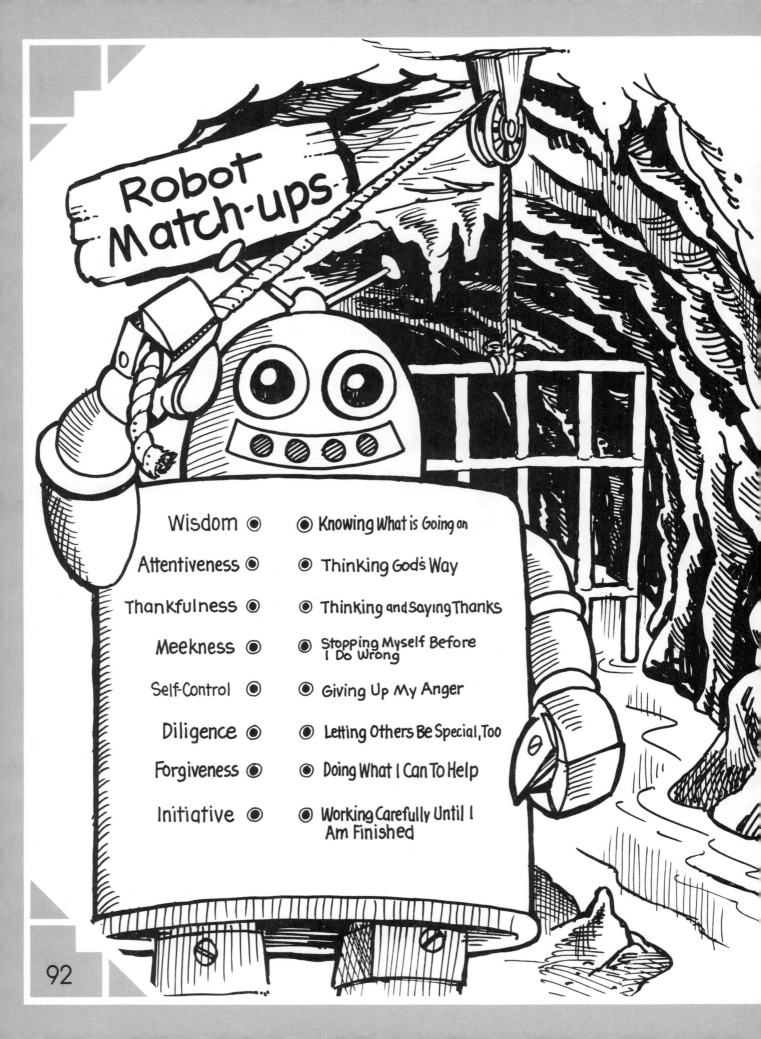

Robot Match-ups

Wisdom ● ● Knowing What is Going on

Attentiveness ● ● Thinking God's Way

Thankfulness ● ● Thinking and Saying Thanks

Meekness ● ● Stopping Myself Before I Do Wrong

Self-Control ● ● Giving Up My Anger

Diligence ● ● Letting Others Be Special, Too

Forgiveness ● ● Doing What I Can To Help

Initiative ● ● Working Carefully Until I Am Finished

A Prayer to our Great God

_____

- -

_____

- -

_____

- -

_____

- -

_____

- -